Believe-in Your Special Gift

S.V. Davies

Heddon Publishing

First edition published in 2018 by Heddon Publishing.
Copyright Sue Davies 2018, all rights reserved.

No part of this book may be reproduced, adapted, stored in a retrieval system or transmitted at any time or by any means mechanical, electronic, photocopying, recording or otherwise, without the prior, written permission of the author.

The information in this book should not be used for diagnosing or treating any health condition. You should always consult a trained medical professional before undertaking any form of exercise as this can affect medical conditions or medication. The author and publisher disclaim any liability directly or indirectly from the use of this book.

ISBN 978-1-9995963-7-8

Written and illustrated by Sue Davies

Cover and borders illustrated by
Catherine Clarke | @catherineclarke

HEDDON PUBLISHING
www.heddonpublishing.com
www.facebook.com/heddonpublishing
@PublishHeddon

We each are born with a special gift to share in this world,
individually and uniquely wrapped:
different shapes, shades, sizes, all equally beautiful!

Let's start the journey together,
learning to celebrate our own and others' unique wrapping,
to begin to look inside and find that special gift we were born to share.

Welcome to Believe-in your Special Gift x

By S.V. Davies

I would like to introduce you to my Believe-in Your Special Gift class:

Astro · Mira · Crispin

Ciana · Terran · Xaria

My class wanted to share with you what makes this time of year very magical for all of us and what could be hidden inside each of us; our very own Special Gift! They have explored how to find their own gifts through breathing, physical movements, relaxation and mindfulness.

We all have things in common but there are also things which make us unique and different from each other. Hidden within us all is a unique gift, given to us to share with others and the world. But what could that gift be? How do we find it? And is it the gift what you want it to be? Maybe we can find these things out together.

While you are learning and practising yoga movements, these rules will help to keep you and your body safe:

- Use your body, your mind and your breath together. It sounds like a lot to think about but with a bit of practice you'll soon get used to it.

- Follow the instructions as closely as possible. There is no 'perfect' movement, just safe or unsafe movements. The instructions will help to make sure you are acting in a safe way.

- STOP if you feel any pain or discomfort. Listening to, respecting, and looking after your body puts you in control. Don't do anything that can hurt yourself physically, emotionally or mentally.

- Be yourself. It is important to remember that we are all different. Your body is yours, and unique to you! Try not to copy or push your body to be like anyone else. Yoga is about living in your body and accepting and loving what your body can do. This shows yourself TRUE respect as your body is individual and amazing as it is!

- Use this book in the right way for you. You may prefer some exercises to others, and there may be some you don't want to practise. That is absolutely fine. It is your body, so practise what is right for you.

- Practice! The more you practise the activities and exercises in this book, the more you will understand your body so that you can find the special gift inside yourself.

- HAVE FUN and ENJOY YOURSELF! This story is all for You!

Sue x

Hi! It's Mira.

I have been asked to welcome you as part of the Present Gang! (Crispin's idea) so welcome! We are going to show you what we learned this term: some really good, fun activities and exercises that will help bring this holiday season to life! So please join in and share this book and activities so that we can all enjoy, learn to unwrap our gifts, and be confident to share them with each other!

We have each chosen to show you a breathing exercise we learned during our classes. Our BREATH is one of the most precious gifts we have! By trying these exercises, we can connect with it and remember how precious it is as it is our life force.
When we are showing you our chosen movement please try to remember to follow the rules; this way we keep our bodies safe from injury and we have fun!

You can practise all our movements and explore all of the activities at any time of the year.

Some of these activities are mindfulness activities, which help us think about ourselves, what makes us unique and special, and also some relaxing exercises which help us become better connected to who we are.

Terran here!

At the start of every class, we practise 'tuning into' ourselves. Tuning in helps us focus and listen to our mind, body and breath in that moment. For some it can be difficult and sometimes uncomfortable at the start as we are slowing our bodies down to listen. With practice it becomes a lot easier and now we can tune in any time really easily.

To tune in, when you are ready, find a comfortable position, sitting on a mat or chair, and close your eyes (if that is comfortable for you - if not, try looking down). This helps us focus inside, instead of looking around and risking becoming distracted.

First, we each have a monkey mind that likes to jump from thought to thought like a monkey jumping through the trees! For one minute, just notice how many thought branches your monkey is leaping to today.

It is now my turn to introduce the next part.

It's Astro by the way!

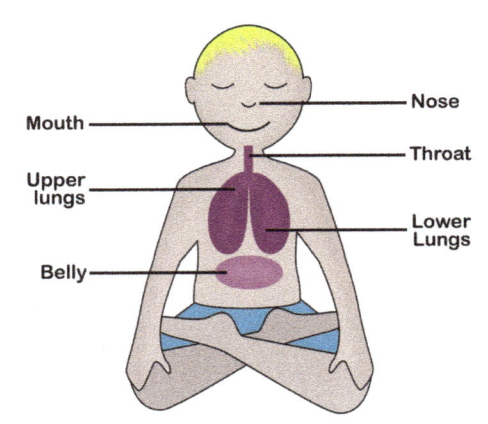

Next, let's see if you can notice where you can feel your breath.
It can be in your nose, your throat, chest or belly. Don't worry if you don't feel anything straight away... it takes time.
Now, see if it is warm or cool air you feel.

Lastly, you could just notice how your body feels,
are there any aches, pains or sensations?

Are there any feelings or emotions that you can recognise?
Where do you feel them in your body?
Again, don't worry if you don't feel anything straight away.

Tuning in is a good way of looking inside.
Every time we do, it will be different,
as we are constantly changing.

Hi I'm Ciana!

We all think that holiday seasons are magical. Some of us like Xaria go away on holiday; Astro and Mira spend time with their families; I visit lots of friends I don't see often; and Crispin attends a holiday club. We all celebrate in different ways.
When we discussed what feelings or emotions we have over the holidays these are just some that we found:

Happiness   *Loneliness*   *Joy*   *Hope*   *Sadness*
Argumentative   *Disappointment*   *Love*   *Anxiety*   *Fear*
Excitement   *Envy*   *Gratitude*   *Greed*

Some of these emotions can make us feel yukky and we sometimes fight or try to hide them. The teacher said that every emotion teaches us something - even the yukky ones!
 We did this exercise where we became our own 'inn-keepers' and each emotion became a 'visitor' or 'guest'. Like any good inn-keeper, we can learn to welcome every emotion, even the yukky ones, with a "Hello and welcome."
During the time an emotion is with us, if we get to know it and where in our 'inn' it is staying, if we start speaking to it we can find out why it is visiting, then we have a chance to discover what it can teach us about a situation or even ourselves.

The inn keeper is an exercise adapted from the mindfulness poem **The Guest House** written by Jellaludin Rumi in the 13th century.

Xaria will now introduce what to do next…

Xaria here!

To learn to become our inn-keepers we:-

1) Need to recognise the emotion visiting. We can also notice the effect it has: it may be visible (e.g. through facial expression), or invisible - we can feel it inside our bodies; it might change our behaviour towards others. When you recognise an emotion – any emotion – take a moment to acknowledge, say hi and give it a tag or label.

2) Next, we really need to put this emotion or guest into the register. We do that by accepting and feeling that emotion. This can be very difficult and even too much if the emotion is BIG or yukky. It's those emotions we sometimes don't want to register and feel and instead want to push them away, hide them or even try to ignore them. None of those things unfortunately will get rid of this guest. Instead, it may stop even longer or get even BIGGER! Just to be heard. So, when you're ready, maybe sit comfortably and ask some questions: What has made me feel this emotion? Where do I feel it? Is the emotion linked to a person or situation? What can I learn from it?

3) Once we have felt the emotion, and know why it came to visit us and what it can teach us, its stay will come to an end and it will be free to leave. Emotions never stop for long, they can't! The body can't sustain any emotion for a long time, even if you feel it may stay forever! It won't. Once it has had its say it's then time to leave and we again as inn-keepers are in control. We can even thank the emotion for its visit and wish it farewell and goodbye with kindness and love.

This sometimes can feel really hard and difficult, when you first start registering your emotions. If at any time you feel overwhelmed by any and they feel so BIG then try some deep breathing. Breathe in 1, 2, 3, 4 then breathe out 1, 2, 3, 4, 5… this will help relax you. Give it a go!

Now, let's go, exploring some topics together, finding and sharing the magic in this time of year. We may just find our special gifts, too!

The Universe and Us by Astro

Planet Earth is home to us all, yet only a tiny speck of sand within our vast universe! Even though we humans are small, we can find a VAST amount of space within our own minds and bodies. One way to do this is by practising how our breath is connected to the universe! Are you sitting comfortably? Now you can start to focus on your inhales: as we breathe in we are bringing the world's atmosphere into our bodies to sustain us. Focus on this for up to five breaths

Next, focus on your exhales, on how the air you breathe out is now re-entering the atmosphere. Focus on this for five breaths.

We are now going to notice the space within our bodies. As you inhale, just notice how your body, your lungs and rib cage, expand to allow the breath to enter, then notice how that space contracts as your breath leaves. Focus on your body working effortlessly with the atmosphere for another three breaths.

Now I want to share some movements that remind me of the universe and things in it. I love the stars as I like astronomy (which is studying them). Sailors used to be guided by them too! I like them as each is unique and has its own individual position in the sky, and light that shines.

Star

If it is comfortable for you, stand with your legs wide apart, connected to the earth by your feet.

As you inhale, you can stretch your arms wide out to the sides, or diagonally if you are comfortable to do so, making a five-pointed star!

You can try to wiggle your toes and fingers to make your star sparkle and shine.

Twisted Star

Starting from wide-leg standing, breathe in. As you exhale, lean down into a wide-leg forward bend.

You can bend your knees so your hands touch the floor.

As you inhale, run one of your hands up the other arm, across your chest and turn towards the sky, opening your body up to the side into a twist.

Exhale as you roll back down and try on the other side. To come back up to standing, engage your belly towards your back and inhale as you come back up, using your hips.

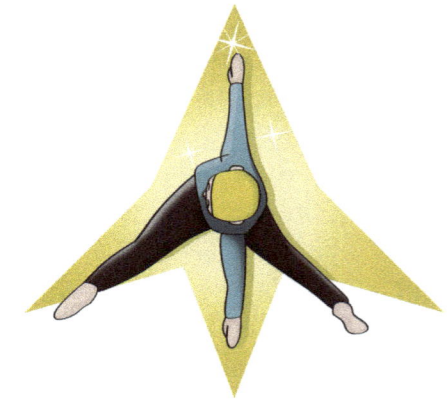

Sound of the Universe!

Sound is made up of waves which resonate outwards into the world. The sound 'Om' or 'AUM' is believed to be the sound of the universe. This sound can make waves to resonate within our bodies and is a way of bringing the universe within ourselves!

Why don't you see if you can hum along with the universe?

Sitting in a comfortable position, take some nice breaths in and out of your nose.

• The first sound we make as we breathe out is the letter 'R', like 'Arrrrrrrrrrrrrr'. As you take two normal breaths, notice where you felt the vibration.

• The next sound is 'O', like 'Ohhhh' – again, take two normal breaths. Where did you feel that vibration?

• The last sound is 'M', like 'Mmmmmmm' – again, as you breathe normally, register where you felt this.

• Let's try putting it all together: 'Arrrrr, Ohhhh, Mmmmm,' and notice how that feels.
If you practise it enough, you may start to feel like your whole body is being massaged!

Star Activity

We really enjoyed this activity and I hope you enjoy it, too! Below is a five-pointed star. On each point, think of something that you really enjoy: a hobby or something you love, and put it on a point of the star, until you have five precious things that make you light you up just like a STAR and shine bright! Maybe you can share this with your friends and family.

Winter by Crispin

Hi! I'm Cris (short for Crispin) and I have been given winter as my theme. I do like winter – especially snow, and that it's the time of year that everything and everyone slows down. With fires, hot chocolate and snuggling up nice and warm, just like all the little animals hibernating, although my hamster doesn't hibernate! In class, we explored how winter is that much-needed pause between the autumn - where nature has let go - and the beginnings of the new year and spring. My favourite breathing exercise was the Winter's Pause. Let me show it to you:

If you want, you can keep your eyes open but if you are happy to close them, even better. You can focus on your breath. Notice that your inhale is like **spring**, the new beginning of the breath's journey.

Think about your exhale. That is like **autumn**, when nature is letting go.

Now, take a moment to realise that in between the inhale and the exhale there is a short 'pause' that happens automatically; just like **summer**, where the flowers are in full bloom, like our lungs full of air.

There is another 'pause' that happens automatically, between the exhale and the next inhale, where the body is empty of breath. This pause is in readiness and anticipation of the next new 'inhale of life'! This is a lot like winter.

Did you notice the pauses? We don't need to go far to notice that the seasons and nature are within us, in our breath.

For the winter movements I have chosen my ultimate fave things to do (apart from drinking hot chocolate). One pose reminds me of happy family times, when my mum took me skiing - doing Chair Pose is like skiing or like being on a ski lift! Another I like is ice skating (I am not that good at it but enjoy it). I also have something I love to do with my friends: sledging, of course!. See if you like these things too!

My mum loves the winter as much as I do and I was born when it was snowing! I hope you enjoy the movements along with me.

Chair Pose

This is me and mum skiing ... whooosh!

First, maybe try standing in Mountain Pose, where we stand upright and strong.
Standing strong on the floor or skis, ground your feet and legs.
Raise up through your spine. Roll your shoulders back and your arms to the side.
Your head balanced at the very top of your spine.
On an inhale, try raising your arms up
to the sky. As you exhale, imagine there is a chair behind you and you are sitting down on it.
This will be hard work for your thighs but is really good for skiing!
Remember to breathe!
When you have had enough, inhale and raise yourself off the chair, stretching up and back to standing.

Dancer Pose

This is a lovely pose, just like an ice-skater!
First, let's stand up straight in Mountain Pose, again legs nice and strong, shoulders rounded back and down with arms out to the side. Next, bend one of your legs at the knee backwards and reach back to hold on to your ankle.
When you are ready and your standing leg is strong, try bending forwards from the hips.
If still strong you can try lifting your leg gently up and outward.
If you still feel strong and not wobbly, you can try to put your other arm out in front of you into an elegant position.
Anytime you become wobbly, slowly lower back down. You can try the same movement on the opposite side!
This is a balancing posture and with practice your dancer will grow in grace, just like an ice-skater! We can't expect to be a perfect skater first time!

Seated Forward Bend

This reminds me of sledging with my friends.

First, we need to sit on our sledges - sitting on the floor, feet forward, back straight.
Imagine you are holding on to the reins of the sled.
As you inhale, raise the reins up and as you exhale bend forward at the hips.
Looking forwards, you can imagine you're sledging down a hill, twisting and turning or you can lower your head to get some speed and relax into the ride.
At the bottom of the hill, engage your belly to your spine and inhale as you raise your arms back up and come back to sitting!

Doing these movements always makes me feel a lot more festive! Do you feel festive too?

Mindfulness Task

For our mindfulness task we took the time to 'pause'; just like our breath did, nature does as it sleeps. So find a lovely comfortable position, sitting or lying down, and let's look and remember the things you have done over this past year. These could be happy things; sad things; things you achieved; things that you are still working on. This is a good way of just noticing where you are right now and how far you have come, the achievements you have made no matter how small.

I hadn't realised I did so much! Try to complete your assessment during this pause by considering the following:

Over the past year

- *What have I enjoyed? What has gone well?*

- *What has been my favourite moment/s?*

- *What has been difficult?*

- *What has not gone so well? What have I learned?*

Now, let's now look to the coming year. We created our own 'vision board' in class, which shows what we would like for the next year. It can include pictures, drawings, writing, photographs, etc. about hobbies, new interests, holidays, friends, pets, anything! By doing this we are visualising what we would like to see in our lives!

What I would like to happen in the next year

Nature by Terran

I was given the topic of nature, which was a bit weird for me as I never really take much notice of nature and I didn't know where to start. I live in a city and I didn't think there was much nature in a city!

I asked my grandad for help. He made me a chart to tick every time I saw a tree, a flower, a bird, a dog, a cat, or bugs like ladybirds, caterpillars, and bees too! He also explained that nature includes weather and forces like gravity and energy. In one week, I recorded LOTS. I didn't realise that there was so much nature all around me, even in a big city! I even saw plants growing in between buildings and pavements and lots of houses on my way to school have really nice gardens, where lots of different creatures live.

My grandad has a lovely garden, too, and he likes walking. I would like to show you various trees I saw in my chart: some that in winter have let go of their leaves, which my teacher says shows us that letting go is a beautiful part of life. He explained how nature is dependent on us but we are dependent on it, too. Like trees and plants. We rely on these for our oxygen (Astro told me that one). And we rely on bees to pollinate, so we can grow our food, and the ground needs the little tiny insects also! Then trees need us for our carbon dioxide, bees need us to help them, like with growing the right kinds of plants, and the insects need us to protect them. My grandad said that nature is like a woven tapestry, all interlinked, and makes a beautiful picture.

My Breathing Activity

If you want to join me, find a nice place to sit and tune into your breath like we have done before.

• As you inhale, try to fill your belly and lungs up with a full breath. Focus on the air as it goes in and think about the trees and plants that are helping you, giving the oxygen you are inhaling. Give thanks to them as you do this.

• When you exhale, breathe out from your lungs then your belly, until all air is expelled. Focus on this air and how it can help keep those plants and trees alive. Send love out to all of nature.

The movements about nature were easy to find. I would like to show you various trees I saw in my chart: some that in winter have let go of their leaves, which my teacher says that shows us that letting go is a beautiful part of life. There are also trees that don't let go or shed their leaves, and some of us have these in our homes for Christmas. My last movement is Child's Pose, as a lot of nature is snuggled up sleeping like flowers, plants and small animals that are hibernating.

So please join me when you are ready, to welcome nature in.

Tree

From standing Mountain Pose, imagine your toes are the roots of the tree and imagine they are going deep into the ground.

To make the trunk of the tree, our legs need to be really strong and we do this by engaging the muscles of our legs.

All the way up your torso, your belly and chest are open and your spine is straight. This makes for a very strong tree!

When you are ready, see where you can place your foot. The heel of one foot can go: On the top of the other,

Or see if you can lift the sole of your foot onto the inside of your calf muscle (the muscle under your knee),

Or even on to the inside of your thigh muscle (the top part of your leg).

If you find it's too windy and your tree becomes wobbly, come down to the position before and regain your strength.

Let's see what type of trees you can be now we can do it…

Tree that has shed its leaves   **Trees that are evergreen, just like a Christmas tree!**

Child's Pose

Time to rest, just like I always want to do in the mornings!

If you want to, start by kneeling, with your bottom back on your feet, then roll down and curl up.

We can put our hands out in front of us or behind us, see which you like better.

Imagine and enjoy nature's pause and rest

In our classes we learned that there is also a nature of 'us'; our bodies, our likes and dislikes and our personalities.

They are the things that make me ME! and you YOU!

Get comfy and draw, colour, write anything from family around you - hobbies, scars, birth marks, hair colour, eye colour - anything that makes you fantastically YOU!

You can share this with friends and family.

Notice first the similarities to your friends', then notice any differences there are. Similarities make us aware that we are all the same as humans and all connected. Differences make us one of a kind - unique!

Nature doesn't compare itself. A tree, a flower or a dog is just 'being' itself. How silly would it be if a tree said 'ooh you have a big fat trunk'? or a dog says 'my tail wags better than yours!'. It is only us humans that compare and pick out differences and then become mean or cause hurt.

If we learn from nature and become more mindful, become human 'beings', we can learn to accept and be comfortable with who we are inside and out. We can also become mindful with others and accept them for who they are!. Accepting ourselves and each other in this way means never needing to compare, just like nature.

Nobody else can ever be ME!! Ty x

Light by Ciana

Hi folks, I was glad I was given this topic. I immediately thought about lots of things that I can use as my movements.

The natural sources of light we have are the sun, the moon, stars, lightning, and the natural phenomenon of the Aurora Borealis (the northern lights), which I hope to go and see one day, and in space the supernova! There are even some animals and plants that can create their own light, like fireflies and jellyfish and mushrooms! Artificial light comes from things like candles, oil lamps, fire, fireworks, flashes from cameras, light bulbs and tree lights.

I have read that too much of artificial light is pollution, like in cities. It affects the sky, meaning birds can get confused and cannot see the sky or stars. Sometimes this happens to me when someone takes my picture as the light blinds me and makes my vision go funny. It's scary. My name means 'light' (I think that is why the teacher gave this topic to me!) and I would like to invite you to join me in this breathing exercise, where we imagine different lights as we breathe. You can sit or lie down.

As you breathe in, imagine little particles of light entering your body and travelling all around. With every inhale, these particles grow and we start to feel warm and glow from within.
On every exhale, send this light out into the world.

I love the yoga moves that I have chosen as they remind me to feel the light, and the warmth that it gives me and my body. I invite you to join in with my sequence if you would like.

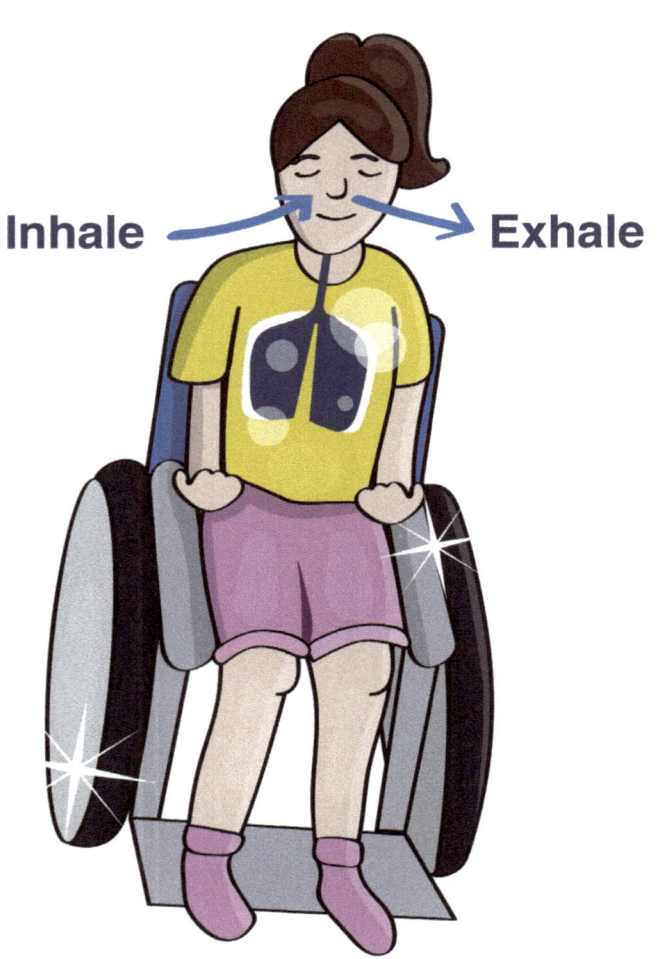

The Moon

Either seated (like me) or standing, be tall and strong, like a mountain.
As you breathe in, you can raise your arms up over your head.
To make your moon shine, all you need to do is exhale as you lean from the waist across to one side then inhale as you bring your body back to centre.
Repeat this to the other side.
We can now try holding the moon's shape for a few breaths; if you wish to try, you can do so on either side.

Candle

We need a wall for this, or a chair.

Come to lying on the floor.
We need to sit first, with our side by the wall or chair.
Then lie down on your side, which leaves your bottom by the wall.

Bend your knees onto your chest and roll onto your back.
You can then lift your legs up to rest against the wall or on the chair seat.
I have help with this but once in this position it is lovely! It is really relaxing and helps my mind calm after a busy day!
To come out, we do it in reverse so, hugging knees, roll then slowly, gently sit up.

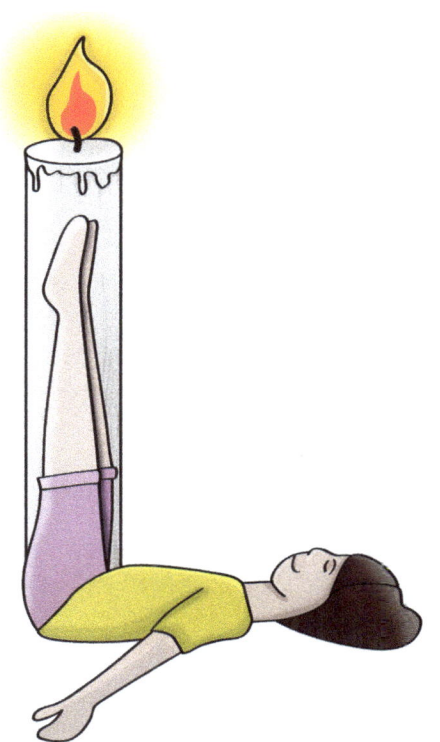

Gift/Present by Xaria

I am very excited to get this topic as I love presents!! My favourite part of getting a gift from friends or family is to try to guess what is inside the wrapping!

That is what makes it special! We don't know what could be hidden inside. We can try to guess from the outside: by its size, its shape, the wrapping, but we still don't know. I don't know about you but I also feel a present to try and find out what it is. I shake it, squidge it: anything to give me any clue to what surprises it could hold.

We did a fantastic mindfulness exercise which we will do first if that's ok? The teacher said that we are like a present, we were born as a gift for our parents, families and to the world, and each of us is wrapped in our own unique wrapping, made up of different body shapes and sizes, facial features, hair and eye colour, skin shades, sound, and clothing, much like a present and its wrapping.

So we needed to think of ourselves as a present. You can use the space below to design a present that represents you: again, any shape or size, with wrapping of any kind, of any pattern, colour, texture… anything! Make it you.

Did you know that being mindful is being present in the moment? So as you're doing this mindfulness exercise you can become present in the present! Get it? Hahaha.

When we meet someone new we can sometimes think we can guess what they are like by the way they look, dress, speak or act. This is called stereotyping. Much like we were told that a cover of a book does not tell the story inside, the wrapping of a present does not give a clue as to what gift is inside, and somebody's appearance does not tell us what that person is like.

To know the story of a book, read it. To find the gift inside of a present, start to unwrap it. The same goes with people; don't judge others on your first impressions, get to know them, see how they make you feel, to know what someone is like.

Being mindful is being present in the moment, not living in the past or worrying about the future but living now. That is why today is a gift! The most precious gift of all. Life!

When we tune in, we focus on what it feels like to be alive and within our bodies right now! If you would like to join me:

Let's tune into our minds… see what your monkey is doing,

Then focus on your body… noticing any feelings or sensations.

Finally, tune into your breath… in, out… in, out.

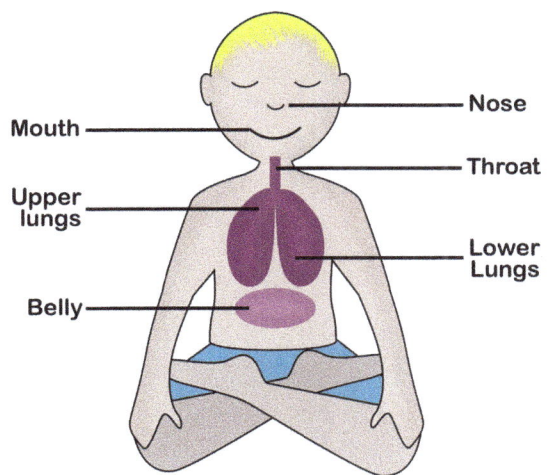

All this is where the gift of life lives.

The movements I want to share with you are the ones we did in class, making our bodies into lots of different shapes! Just like the presents and gifts we can receive from loved ones, which can be many different shapes and sizes! That's what makes them exciting!!

I invite you to join me… Let's try **Triangle** first!

Triangle

Let's stand in Mountain Pose, and take a big step forwards!
Our hips are open to the side.
Then we raise our arms just like we were going into a Warrior movement but instead we lift up from our waist and bend towards the front foot.
We need to keep our backs nice and flat so just rest your hand on your leg wherever is comfortable for you.
This is Triangle! Let's take a couple of breaths here then on an inhale rise back up and try it on the other side!

Box Shape

To become a **Box Shape...**

First let's come down onto the floor. You can do this two ways:
One is just on all fours but we can make a bigger box if we start by sitting down.
Place your hands behind you, fingers pointing towards your bottom.
Knees up and feet on the floor, on an inhale you raise your bottom off the floor until your head, shoulders, belly, hips and knees are all in a line!
A much bigger box means a much bigger present, right!?
To come out of this position we just exhale and come back down to sitting.

Plank Pose

To make the **Plank Pose**...

We again start off on all fours.
Engage your belly muscles as you take one leg back and come onto your toes.
Then take the other leg back to meet the first one.
In this pose we are keeping our bodies in a straight line from head to toe.
Hold for 1, 2, 3, 4 or 5 breaths and then come back to all fours then curl up into Child's Pose.

Circle

Circle can be either an easy or hard pose.
Easy: we just curl up into a ball, like Child's Pose.
Or we can make a bigger circle (which means a bigger present, obviously!)
We come to lying belly-down on our mats then we reach back with our hands and hold our ankles.
With an inhale we lift our head and chest off the floor, along with our knees, raising up.
It is a very difficult pose and I couldn't lift up for AGES! But I can do it now - not for long but I can!
Exhale to come back down and then go into the lovely curled-up ball in Child's Pose as this stretches your back nicely.

Can you do other shapes with your body?

Which shape did you like making the most?

Easy pose

Hard pose

With our teacher we explored that many of us want to fit in and be the same as our friends, that sometimes we can hide parts of us like our likes, hobbies and things about our lives. We do this sometimes so others might not make fun of them. It can be scary to show these things but being you is all you can be! And being you is the best way to finding that special gift inside.

We also learned about the gifts that we all possess inside, which are universal, to share with our friends, family, and everyone!:

love   empathy   acceptance   compassion
helpfulness   patience   kindness   peace
understanding   openness   friendliness

The more we learn to find these gifts inside ourselves and share them, the better we grow and the nicer the world becomes for everyone. By leaving out some of the things that make us light up or happy we are not showing people who we truly are.

Apart from these universal gifts that we have inside we each have been born with a 'Special Gift' - something inside of us that is totally unique and individually ours. This gift is the one that we have been born to share with the world.

In school we have been learning about famous people's lives; people who are/were writers, singers, scientists, doctors, or inventors, or those that did something truly amazing to change someone's life or make our world better in some way. Ciana asked how we find out what our special gift is. The teacher explained that some people find out really early on what their gift is, where for others it can take until they become an adult to really find their gift. The way we can find our own gift is the way we have been practising within these topics. If we learn to tune into ourselves, to understand what makes us shine, to share who we are and what we like with others, and try new things to find out what we like and don't like, we get to truly know who we are. It is only by knowing and exploring who we are inside that we will find that 'Special Unique Gift'.

I guess this is one present I will have to wait to unwrap fully! But it will be worth the wait! Astro has said his will be walking on Mars! Typical, hahaha.

Blessings with Mira

I am the last of the group to share what I have learned in the Believe-in classes and I am going to tell you about blessings. During the classes we learned to appreciate and love our breath, with lots of activities. I didn't realise how precious breathing is. We just do it without thinking, don't we?

My breathing exercise for you is one which looks difficult but once you know it it's really good! It's a special technique called alternate nostril breathing (in India this is called Nadi Shodhana). It's my favourite!

Are you sitting comfortably? If so, you need your thumb and first finger.

First, find which nostril is clearer; to do this we close off one nostril with our finger on the outside of our nose (not inside as that is GROSS!) and breathe in and out. Check the other and decide which one is clearer.
Start the exercise with the clearer nostril and close off your other nostril with either your finger or thumb pressed onto that side of your nose.
Breathe in through the open nostril…
Close off both nostrils with both your finger and thumb for two seconds…
Open up the other nostril and breathe out…
Breathe back in, through that second nostril…
Close off both nostrils with your finger and thumb again for two seconds…
Release the first nostril and breathe out once more…
That is one round of alternate nostril-breathing. Try it again up to four more times.

This exercise helps connect both hemispheres of your brain, it regulates your oxygen, clears your mind, and emotions too! I now do this a couple of times in the morning and at night and if I am having a stressful day.

The movements I have chosen for blessings are: **Mountain Pose**, which is standing; **Lotus**, which is sitting, and **Savasana**, which is lying down. I have lots of fun doing lots of yoga but these are the movements I can really think of blessings as they are more still and thoughtful. I like doing these and reflecting on the day, and the people and places in my life.

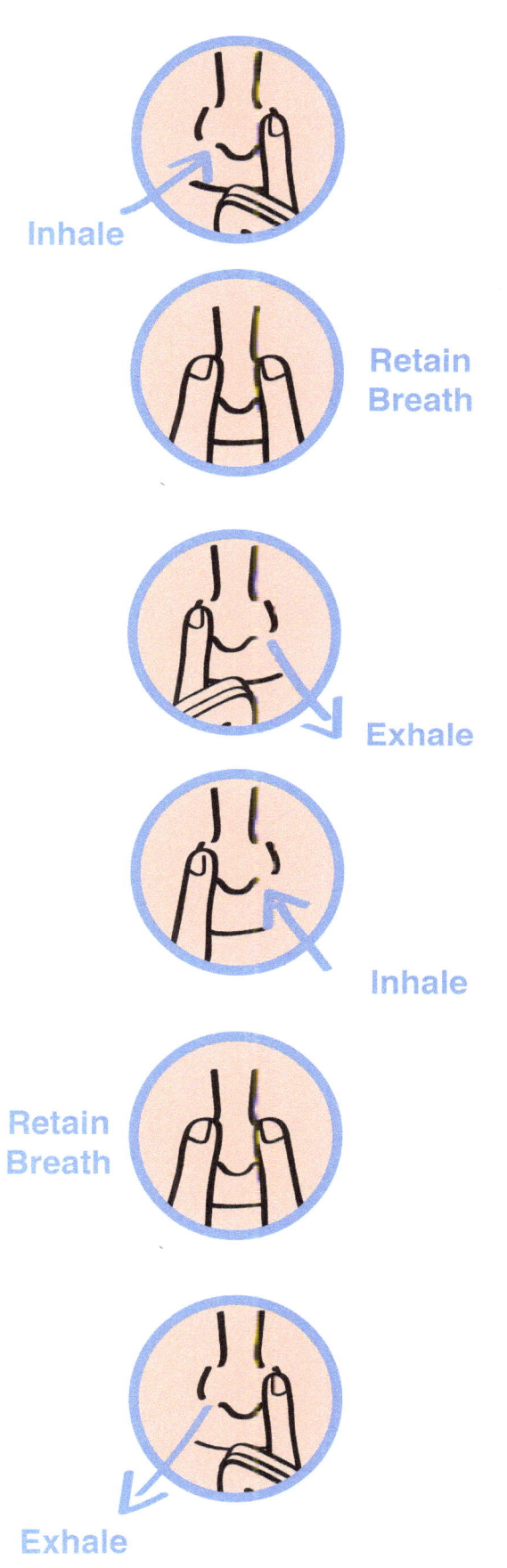

Mountain Pose

Join me if you wish in Mountain Pose, standing tall and strong.
To do this properly we spread our toes and grip the mat.
Then let's engage our calf and thigh muscles in our legs.
Tighten our belly muscles and straighten up our spines so we are standing tall.
Shoulders can open when we roll them backwards, arms out to the side.
Lastly, our head sits comfortable at the top of the spine.
We can now try closing our eyes if that is comfortable - if not, we can look downward.

Whilst in this pose bring to mind any physical places in your life that you are thankful for. Places that you feel strong, grounded, safe and secure.

Give thanks to them as you stand here and feel how they and Mountain Pose make you feel strong, grounded and safe.

Lotus

Whilst in this pose bring to mind the people in our lives that have supported us, love us and who inspire us and in bringing them to mind being grateful and blessed to have them in our lives.

Easy Pose

Half Lotus

Full Lotus

Savasana

Lastly, come to lying down in Savasana, which I found out is also called Corpse Pose! That's not a nice name for a pose!

I guess this pose is about becoming really, really still, lying down. So come to lying on your mat, bed or the floor and when you are comfortable start to relax each part of your body, moving from your toes upward. With every out breath, relax your legs, arms, torso and let them go floppy, like cooked spaghetti! (We found that funny when the teacher said that!)

Once fully relaxed and floppy, bring to mind yourself. Picture and feel yourself lying down right here and now. Which parts of your body are touching the floor? What is your breath doing? What thoughts is your monkey jumping to?

Feel what it is like to be alive right now within your body; the sensations you are experiencing just lying still. Being thankful for being alive. You can stay in this position for up to five minutes.

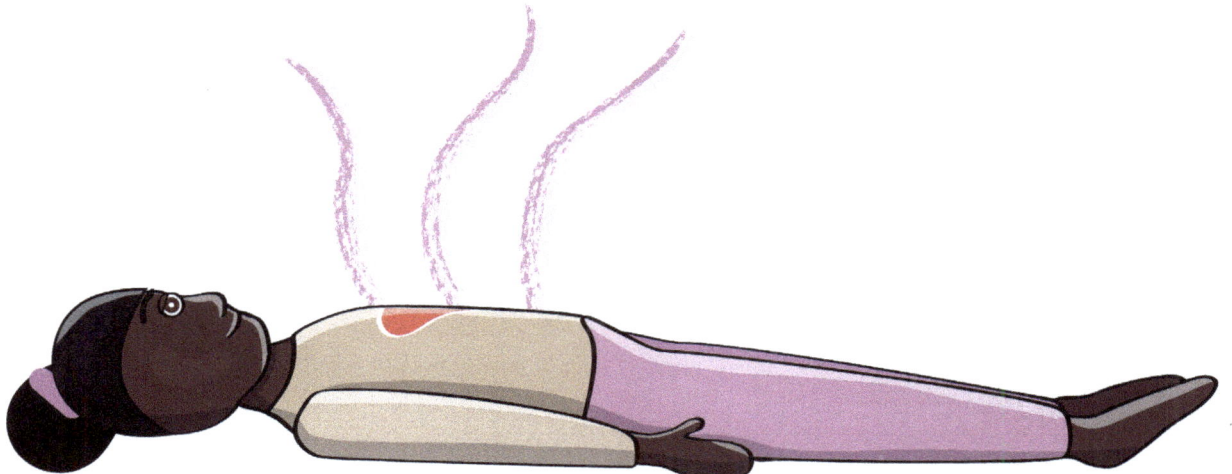

Which position made you feel most relaxed and able to focus on blessings? Remember, this can change every time you do these movements.

What did you discover:
About places?
About the people in your life?
About yourself and your body?

We were asked to complete a gratitude diary every day, twice a day! I thought it would be really hard as thinking like this was really new to me.

Every morning before getting up we needed to try to name up to three things we were grateful for at the start of a new day. Then every evening, before going to bed, we needed to think about the day and try to name up to three things we were grateful for that day.

Now, being grateful doesn't always mean nice things: sometimes we can be grateful for challenges, or something difficult that happened; that we learned something new about others or ourselves. Some days might be easier to think of things to be grateful for and some days can be really hard. Sometimes I repeated things I was grateful for, but that's ok! The teacher said that repeating blessings, no matter how big or small, honours the impact that they have in your life. See if you would like give it a go.

Here are some examples in case your mind goes blank:-

'I am grateful for my dog waking me up this morning by jumping on my bed as I would have been late for school if it didn't.'

'I am blessed my ankle has healed, I can now play football again!'

'I am grateful for my friends' help in explaining how to do some difficult questions in maths.'

'I am blessed to have such a loving grandad who teaches me about history.'

My Gratitude and Blessings Diary

Day	Morning's Blessings & Gratitudes	Evening's Blessings & Gratitudes
MONDAY		
TUESDAY		
WEDNESDAY		
THURSDAY		
FRIDAY		
SATURDAY		
SUNDAY		

I hope you have enjoyed exploring with my class and all the really interesting movements and exercises that are linked very closely with who we are. They only realised during the classes that the topics they had were the meanings of their names!

Astro means 'universe'.

I love this one, we are all connected in the world and universe. We breathe the same air, and any time we feel lost we can always connect to receive universal energy in our breath, movements and in the space we find within us!

Crispin comes from the meaning 'Crisp', as in snow or cold.

Winter is such a lovely season and Crispin embraces this with a lot of fun! We can learn to embrace every season outside with each other! But also know that the seasons are always with us as we inhale, pause, exhale and pause.

Terran actually means 'nature'!

It is easy to go about our daily lives without noticing the nature that is all around us and more so the nature of who we are!
I am ME and you are YOU! And we can't and don't need to be like anyone else! Learning this helps build self-confidence and also helps us love ourselves. You will find that once we do that, everyone can see us shine!

Ciana is actually 'light'.

We all need light to brighten up the dark. The natural light is so warming and bright, it calms us and also gives us energy. We also have that spark and light inside of us… Astro showed us that it shines when we are around the people and the things that make us happy, our friends and the things we love. This light we share with others.

Xaria (Zaria) has a lovely meaning of 'gift'.

We are all gifts to this world, and Xaria showed us wonderfully how presents come in different sizes, shapes and shades: each beautifully unique and special. We learned that judging something by its wrapping or guessing what something is doesn't actually mean we know what is inside. We learned that we do the same with people, however when we become more mindful and present, we learn to look at things differently and learn to get to know who someone is and not decide by the wrapping alone. Being present in the moment in life, which is the biggest gift we have, can lead us to finding our Special Gifts!

Mira has a beautiful name, meaning 'blessings'.

We are all so busy, children and adults equally, that we sometimes forget to count the blessings we have in our lives right now: our family, our friends, our homes, food, health, movement, breath! Becoming more grateful for the little things we have, no matter how small, every day, can enrich our lives. We can become happier, healthier and more connected, and loved.

Thank you for joining our class. I hope you have enjoyed this book and had fun and learned more about who you are! To celebrate what makes you You! And you find some of the exercises in this book helpful for every day, not just over the winter holidays. I know as a class we did!

Our last task is a relaxation exercise. You may need some help from a parent or carer, to read it to you, or you can play it off our website: www.believe-in.co.uk. Enjoy!

From all of us at Believe-in we wish you a very happy holidays and festive season!

Sue x

If you are happy to do so, lie on your back with either your arms by the side of your body in Savasana, or maybe try with your legs up the wall, in Candle, whichever is more relaxing for you.

You can put a blanket or a fleece over you if you have one in easy reach but don't worry if you don't.

You can close your eyes, or half-close them, whichever is comfortable for you at this time.

Firstly, try to notice how your body feels lying on the earth…
Notice which parts of your body are touching the earth: feet, legs, pelvis, back, arms, hands and head.
You may want to check in with your breathing. Where is your breath right now?
If your body needs it, take a few deep breaths into your belly, and as you breathe out, let your body relax a little more, supported by the earth beneath.

Now, whilst you're lying relaxing, imagine you are that present or gift.
Notice how your wrapping is lying on the floor, the shape it makes.
Feel the wrapping around you, your clothes and blanket.
See if any colour comes to mind that you feel around you. Could that be the colour of your wrapping?

As we know, that is not the full story. As the wrapping opens, we see a lovely, warm natural light that glows out. This light feels like Me! Without having to act or live up to anyone else, enjoy the relaxation of just being you!

As the wrapping opens more, we get to see all the things that make up that glow…
Our hobbies. Sports, maybe; pets; family members; books… see what comes to mind!
Give gratitude for each one and thank them for lighting up your life and being part of you.
Next, as these come out of the gift box, see if you can see anything in there that is uniquely you… that special something. Don't worry if nothing comes up straight away, it can take a long while for us to realise what this special gift actually is!

Along with these lovely things, inside you have that light, you have the feelings of love and peace that surround them.

When we are born, we are special gifts; gifts that are wrapped up in unique wrapping especially for our parents, families, friends… and to the world! As we grow we are told that we need to look, be and act all the same so we lose sight of how unique and special we each truly are.

Stay here for the next few minutes feeling love for who you are inside and out and gratitude and blessings for those gifts you have to share.

When your ready let's bring those lovely feelings back into the world by wiggling your fingers and toes, maybe stretch your arms up and toes down or hug your knees upon hour chest. Make any little movements your bodily would like to slowly wake your body up. Roll.onto your right side if you can whilst you slowly open your eyes. Take a breath or two there before you come back up to sitting

Place your hand on your heart and with a positive word, amen or Namaste or any word you choose send love, light and peace for yourself and everyone!

Namaste x

www.ingramcontent.com/pod-product-compliance
Lightning Source LLC
Chambersburg PA
CBHW041809070526
44586CB00025B/2815